I FOUND MY HORN

By Jonathan Guy Lewis and Jasper Rees

Adapted from the book
by Jasper Rees

SAA Press

Performer	Jonathan Guy Lewis
Director	Harry Burton
Designer	Alex Marker
Lighting Designer	Chuma Emembolu
Stage Manager	Andrew Room

Snippets of the following compositions are heard:

Flanders & Swann: 'An Ill Wind'

A$AP Rocky: 'F**kin Problems'

Williams: 'Arlington' from *JFK*

Handel: 'Hallelujah Chorus' from *The Messiah*

Handel (arr. Agrell): 'Hallelujah Chorus' for eight horns

Sibelius: Symphony no 5

Schubert: Symphony no 9 'The Great C Major'

Mozart: Flute concerto no 1

Mozart: Horn concerto no 3

Lennon and McCartney: 'Sgt Pepper's Lonely Hearts Club Band'

Wagner: Horn call from *Siegfried*

Schumann: Konzertstück

Wagner: 'Liebestod' from *Tristan und Isolde*

Haydn: Symphony no 31 'The Hornsignal'

Bruckner: Symphony no 4 'Romantic'

Mahler: Symphony no 7

Beethoven: Horn sonata

Strauss: Horn concerto no 1

Barry: James Bond theme

Rossini: *Le Rendez-vous de Chasse*

Glière: Horn concerto

Williams: 'Funeral Pyre for a Jedi' from *Star Wars: Return of the Jedi*

Wagner: 'The Ride of the Valkyries' from *Die Walküre*

Mozart/Davis/Lombida: Rondo alla Mambo

BIOGRAPHIES

PERFORMER | JONATHAN GUY LEWIS

Jonathan is an award-winning actor, writer and director who also works as a teacher, mentor and coach. Theatre includes: *A View from the Bridge* (Touring Consortium); *The Herbal Bed* (Royal & Derngate, touring); *A Few Good Men* (Theatre Royal Haymarket); *An Inspector Calls* (Aldwych); *Peer Gynt* (National); *Alphabetical Order* and *Elephants* (Hampstead); *Absent Friends* Watford Palace); *Protest/ Mountain Hotel/ Green Wash* and *Myth, Propaganda, and Disaster in Nazi Germany and Contemporary America* (Orange Tree). TV includes: *Soldier Soldier, London's Burning* and *Coronation Street* as well as *Vincent, Skins Redux, Endeavour, Desperados, Silent Witness, Sea of Souls, Holby, Heartbeat, Casualty*. He is also the author of the military-themed plays *Our Boys, Soldier On* and *Tunnel at the End of the Light*, and a trilogy about the state of the nation's education including *A Level Playing Field* and *The Be All and End All.* He is artistic director of the Soldiers' Arts Academy.

DIRECTOR | HARRY BURTON

Harry has been acting and directing for approaching forty years. His directing credits include: *The Lover* (Bridewell); *The Room* (Royal Court); *The Dumb Waiter* (West End); *Quartermaine's Terms* (Windsor); *Where I Come From* (Kentucky Rep); *The Leisure Society* (Trafalgar Studios); *What The Butler Saw* (associate director, Vaudeville); *Casualties* (Park Theatre); *Barking in Essex* (Wyndham's); *God of Carnage* (Copenhagen); *Parzival* (Sharpham House); *Positive* (Park Theatre); *Blue on Blue* (Tristan Bates); *Madame Butterfly* (Cadogan Hall); *Spring* and *The Last Dance* (Frontier Theatre); *Out There on Fried Meat Ridge Road* (White Bear/Trafalgar Studios); *Art, Truth and Politics* (with Mark Rylance, Harold Pinter Theatre); *The Dogwalker* (Jermyn Street); Harold Pinter's *The Dwarfs* (White Bear); *Ashes to Ashes* (BBC Radio); *Working with Pinter* (Channel 4); *Thinspiration* (Channel 4).

AUTHOR | JASPER REES

Jasper is an arts journalist and author.
His books include *I Found My Horn: One
Man's Struggle with the Orchestra's Most
Difficult Instrument* (published in the US as
A Devil to Play), *Bred of Heaven: One
Man's Quest to Reclaim His Welsh Roots*
and *Let's Do It: The Authorised Biography
of Victoria Wood*. He has also edited
*Victoria Wood Unseen on TV: Sketches,
Songs, Stand-up and Other Rarities*.

THE PRODUCERS WOULD
LIKE TO THANK THE FOLLOWING:

Dave Lee, Cal Fell, Dan Thomason, Sara Hill,
Joe Hill and Adam Morane-Griffiths

*In fond memory of
Kendall Betts and Lowell Greer*

I FOUND MY HORN: A History

Jasper Rees resumed the French horn in 2004 on the cusp of his fortieth birthday. Attending the British Horn Society's annual festival, held that year in Southampton, he took part in a seventy-strong massed horn blow performing an eight-part version of the Hallelujah Chorus. At the following festival, held a year later in the Guildhall School of Music and Drama in London, he performed the second and third movement of Mozart's third horn concerto, K.447, accompanied on the piano by his old horn teacher. The resulting book was published by Weidenfeld & Nicolson in January 2008 and abridged for Radio 4's Book of the Week.

Jonathan Guy Lewis, also a lapsed horn player, heard it and suggested collaborating on a one-man stage version. Harry Burton joined as director. The play was premiered at the Aldeburgh Fringe Festival in June 2008. It later enjoyed a run at the Tristan Bates Theatre in the West End, and in 2009 had runs at the Orange Tree in Richmond, the Minerva in Chichester and Hampstead Theatre. In addition there were one-off performances at many festivals, while in 2011 there was a student production at Cambridge University.

In 2014 a new draft of the play was performed in a month-long run at the Trafalgar Studios. A key change was to the play's opening. Previously a spotlight would go up on a nearly naked Jasper, trapped in the throes of a performance-anxiety nightmare. Only the bell of the horn protects his modesty. Now the play began more reflectively as he enters the attic where his past life awaits. This version expanded on the character of Daniel, and turned Jasper's horn into a talking character (which, hailing from Brno, speaks with a Czech accent). The following year, the show was performed at the International Horn Society in Los Angeles.

I Found My Horn was revived in 2023 at the White Bear Theatre in Kennington, then at the Riverside Studios in Hammersmith.

The Lapsed Horn Player as Mythic Hero
by Harry Burton

'Takes bollocks of Sheffield steel to play that thing in public. It's the French horn, Jasper! Takes no prisoners. What do you want to put yourself through that for?' The speaker is Dave Lee in the stage version of *I Found My Horn*, adapted from Jasper Rees's book about his quest for renewed self-belief and a creative rite of passage (otherwise known as navigating a mid-life crisis). But for devoted lovers of myth and folk tale, Dave is not merely an entertainingly earthy character in Jasper's story; he's an archetypal presence essential to any mythic telling of the Hero's Journey: an ally, a sage, a mentor, an Elder, and a King (in fact the word 'mentor' comes direct from *The Odyssey*, where Mentor was a wise friend to Odysseus). Dave is a master of the impossible craft to which the desperate Jasper is belatedly applying himself. In his ripe phrase about Sheffield steel Dave crystallises into a single image the sheer lunacy of Jasper's heroic mission. Sheffield steel is mythic stuff indeed, and as a world-class horn master – and a northener – Dave knows what he's talking about. But like a true mentor he doesn't make the Hero's decision for him. Left to figure it out, Jasper realises what every authentic Hero must, that he is certainly damned if he risks everything to continue the journey, and damned all the more if he doesn't.

Myths are the storehouse of eternal wisdom put aside by our ancestors to assist us in difficult times. They teach us that at the crucial moment on a quest the Hero realises that despite being determined, even willing to die if necessary, he or she simply hasn't the wisdom required to succeed in the challenge. At that moment the Hero has to risk everything by asking for help. To remain silent is to fail. To ask for help is to risk mockery and rejection. But ask the right person, and in the right way, and the story can continue, and the Hero is no longer alone.

To our own considerable peril, we haved demoted the word 'myth' to mean something that is fundamentally untrue. But myths probably emerged at around the same time that we figured out how to make and contain fire. It's the job of myths to make the world meaningful. In losing touch with our ancient mythic imagination we have fallen into passivity and victimhood, experiencing the world as random and meaningless. By shaping his experience into a story, Jasper turned a difficult phase of his life into a song that can nourish others. At the end of the great myths, the Hero returns to the community with a blessing to share in the form of wisdom and experience. It's that nourishment that an audience longs for, and that theatre in our challenging times can provide.

THE HORN: Some Facts

- According to scientists at the University of Ulm, the universe exists in the shape of a horn.

- The horn's best-known biblical cameo is at Jericho. Its first is as the heavenly instrument which summons Moses up Mount Sinai.

- The horn was integral to the culture of the Celts, Romans, Vikings and Normans. It has a starring role in *La Chanson de Roland*, the oldest surviving major work of French literature.

- The earliest image of a fully-circular horn is on a 15th century misericord in Worcester Cathedral.

- In Venice in 1639 the hunting horn made its operatic debut in Cavalli's *Le Nozze di Tete e di Peleo*. The horn was first heard in an English orchestra in 1717 with Handel's *Water Music*.

- The earliest known instance of a female horn player is the duetting wife of a Mr Charles, who toured Europe in the 1740s.

- Rossini, Brahms and Strauss were all the sons of horn players.

- Vincent DeRosa, who played on countless Hollywood soundtracks, is the most recorded horn player in history. He began working in Los Angeles in 1936. Seventy years on he was still playing on *The Simpsons*.

- The horn was the first orchestral instrument to be granted a solo by the Beatles. After 'For No One' on *Revolver*, it appeared in ten further Beatles songs: 'A Day in the Life' (two horns); 'Sgt Pepper's Lonely Hearts Club Band' (four); 'Good Morning Good Morning' (one); 'I Am The Walrus' (three); 'Hey Jude' (two); 'Martha My Dear' (one); 'Good Night' (one); 'Golden Slumbers'/'Carry That Weight' (four); 'The End' (four).

- Dennis Brain's restored single B flat Alexander horn is on display alongside the horns of his father Aubrey and his uncle Alfred at the Royal Academy of Music.

- The current record for the largest ensemble of horn players was set in 2019 at the 51st International Horn Symposium in Ghent where 402 players performed 'Des Sons Animés' by Dirk Brossé, who also conducted.

PLAYING THE HORN: A Guide to Survival

Monsieur Ponté, first French horn player to the King of Prussia, was engaged to play a concerto at the oratorio. He said to Madame Mara in German, 'My dear friend, my lips are so parched with fear, that I am sure I shall not make a sound in the instrument; I would give the world for a little water or beer to moisten my lips.' Madame Mara replied in German, 'There is nobody here to send; and yet if I knew where to get something for you to drink, I would go myself.' During their dialogue, I was standing at the fireside; and addressing Madame Mara in German, I said, 'Madame, I should be sorry for you to have that trouble, and I sit lazy by; I will, with great pleasure, go and get Monsieur Ponté some Porter.' I instantly dispatched a messenger for a foaming pot; and as soon as it arrived, I presented it to the thirsty musician, in the nick of time, for he was called on to play his concerto just at this moment . . .

Michael Kelly, *Reminiscences of the King's Theatre and
Theatre Royal Drury Lane* (1826)

Why is the horn so difficult to play? In contrast to, for example, the piano, where production of its individual notes is taken care of by the keyboard and hammer mechanism, the horn demands that each note must be formed using the lips and the breath in a way which does not come naturally at all. In fact, the instrument itself is of little help to the player. Anyone who can coax music from the horn can generally get a similar result from a few metres of garden hosepipe or even a teapot. The horn, being topologically equivalent to a length of drainpipe, acts only as a specialised resonator. The lips of a horn player are framed by the ring of the mouthpiece in a crude approximation of the way a singer's vocal cords are framed by the larynx. Pushing air between the lips is what gets the air vibrating. Whereas a singer's mouth will resonate and thus amplify any frequency at which the vocal cords vibrate, a horn will only do this from the lips at a few precise frequencies, which are known as harmonics. It is only possible to make the horn ring out beautifully if the pitch at which the lips choose to 'sing' exactly matches that of one of the harmonics. If there is even the slightest mismatch you get farm noises. If you get it right, it's simply the best sound there is. Getting it right is next to impossible.

Pip Eastop, 'Horn identity', *Classical Music* (2008)

'I AM IN LOVE!'
*Photograph:
Gavin Watson*

'Maybe you want we play music again? Like old days?'   *Max Hamilton-Mackenzie*

'My life used to stretch out before me like this vast ocean of opportunity.'
Harry Burton

'Transpose to what, sir?'   Alex Marker

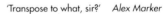

'You play ze whole concerto and you not know ze fingerings?'

Gavin Watson

'I couldn't hit a cow's arse with a banjo!'

Alastair Muir

'Find the sweet spot.'   *Alastair Muir*

'Did you hear those trills?'   *Gavin Watson*

'You've got to have fun on the horn.'   *Tristram Kenton*

I FOUND MY HORN

Published in association
with Soldiers' Arts Academy Press, 2023

Printed in England by CMP Print, Poole, Dorset BH12 4NU

Published by Anna Trussler Design, Devon TQ9 6LB
in association with Soldiers' Arts Academy Press

A catalogue record for this book is available from the British Library

ISBN: PB: 978-1-7394073-0-8

JONATHAN GUY LEWIS AND JASPER REES

I FOUND MY HORN

Adapted from the book
by Jasper Rees

SOUND: Flanders and Swann's 'An Ill Wind'.

A shaft of light as Jasper emerges out of a hatch. A naked bulb dimly lights the dusty attic.

Jasper Do you ever wonder why you're here? What it's all for? We need to know that we mattered, right? To leave a mark; some value in our existence. Of being on this planet at this moment in time. Clock ticking. My name is Jasper. (*Picks up a cricket bat.*) I've just edged past an unbeaten half-century. (*Beat.*) Alright, I'm fifty-six. And I write for a living. I'm a writer. I have high cholesterol, 7.4 . . . not good. Totally unfair, as I don't smoke, don't really drink that much. Don't exercise enough; bad back, L5S1 (also not good). (*Beat.*) This isn't my speed-dating profile, by the way. I'm not trying to come on to you. (*Beat.*) Oh, and I'm getting divorced.

SOUND: A$AP Rocky's 'Fuckin' Problems' suddenly blares from a bedroom on the floor below.

(*Exasperated.*) Daniel. Daniel? DANIEL!? Will you please turn that down!?

'Fuckin' Problems' drops to an irritating thud.

That's Daniel. My son. *Our* son. He's fifteen. Thousands of pounds spent on music lessons, and he chooses to listen to *that*. He's actually a very talented cellist, but you'd never know it. Doesn't practise. I suppose he is a typical teenager. Wears his trousers somewhere south of his buttocks. And he grunts a lot. Oh, and he's always asking for money. Sound familiar?

The trouble is, I don't know where the typical teenage stuff ends and his reaction to the break-up begins: the divorce, and having to sell the house. (*Beat.*) It's a terrible thing to leave your child and your home for the last time. To remove yourself from your life. According to Pamela, the marriage guidance counsellor, 'It takes two to screw up a marriage, Jasper. Not one, not three, but two.' Not that I totally agree with that. But I'll take my 50 percent of the blame. And 100 percent of the bill. She got the equity, I got the debt. Sounds like some terrible country and western song. Life doesn't play out quite the way we expect, does it? (*Beat.*) Anyway, I made a deal with Daniel that I would come to the house today, and that he would help me move my stuff from this attic to the rabbit hutch I now call home. Via the dump. He said he would do this in return for money. So far, though, he hasn't kept his side of the bargain. He still wishes, however, to be given the money. Fatherhood, eh? (*Beat.*)

The music has stopped. Jasper listens, hoping Daniel is coming up to the attic. Silence.

He's not coming, is he?

Assessing his task, Jasper spies something among the clutter.

SOUND: underscore horn solo from John Williams' soundtrack for JFK.

Jasper It's my old French horn! (*Calling downstairs.*) Hey, Dan, come and have a look. It's my old French horn! Dan!?

The front door slams.

Jasper picks up the battered horn case.

I used to play this at school – when I was his age. Only the bravest play the French horn – along with the oboe officially the joint-hardest instrument in the *Guinness Book of Records*. Learnt that in my first lesson, a whole lifetime ago. The bravest – or the stupidest. Why do any of us learn a musical instrument?

My parents used to say, 'You'll thank us when you're older. Music makes us human. It'll give you wings to fly.' I haven't thanked them yet. Abandoning that French horn was more or less the last thing I did before becoming an adult. I was one of those privileged middle-class children who have a musical instrument thrust into their hands. I was ten. It wasn't unlike an arranged marriage, I suppose. Neither of us had much say in the matter. And we stuck it out for seven years before going our separate ways. And since then it's spent the best part of several decades in various attics gathering dust . . . while I've been gathering a certain amount of dust myself.

SOUND: a low knocking.

What was that? Did you hear that? (*Calls.*) Daniel?

SOUND: more persistent knocking. Is it coming from inside the horn case?

(*Spooked.*) Well, I, um . . . Stop fucking about, Daniel! Do you want to go for pizza?

Rapidly retreating to the hatch, he switches off the light and has almost closed the lid when . . .

SOUND: more John Williams horn solo.

Overcome by curiosity he approaches the horn case with the cricket bat as a defensive weapon. Jasper kneels, flicks the catches, lifts the lid and takes out the horn. Light on his face from the case.

Wow! It's . . . cold. Heavy. It's beautiful! (*Reads.*) 'Josef Lídl, Brno.' Where the hell is Brno?

Horn (*Czech accent*) Czechoslovakia.

Jasper What!?

Horn Brno. Is place in Czechoslovakia! You forget this like you forget everything. You forget *me*. You know how long I wait in this stinking rotten case for you to pick me up?

Thirty-nine years, mister. Since you leave me in box they knock down Berlin Wall. They cancel my country. They shoot JR! Thirty-nine years since school music concert – remember?

Jasper panics and tries to stuff the horn back into its case.

Horn Oh no, no, NO! Please don't put me back in box! I can't breathe in box! You don't know what's like! So alone! And dark! And always this terrible gangster *BOOM BOOM!* Motherfucker *BOOM BOOM!* Please, have pity. I beg you.

Jasper Oh, for God's sake this is ridiculous. Please don't – don't do that.

Horn (*imploring*) I help you?

Jasper Help me? What do you mean 'help' me?

Horn Your life go so wrong! Maybe you want we play music again? Like old days?

Jasper How is playing music going to help me?

Horn Everybody want to play music! Is good for soul.

Jasper Yes, I'm sure it is. I'm just a bit preoccupied right now, what with one thing and another.

Horn Oh sure. I get it. But maybe just try? What you got to lose? Ain't nobody here but we chickens. Come on, live a little. Have quick blow.

Jasper Well . . . alright. I suppose a quick blow . . . for old times' sake.

He holds the horn as if to play.

Mouthpiece. Fingers on valves. Hand in the bell. Lips. Embouchure! Yeah, I can't have forgotten everything!

He blows with everything he's got, but an awful noise emerges.

Oh God, I have. I've forgotten everything! (*To Horn.*) So what am I doing wrong? Hmm? Hey? I thought you said you were going to help me? (*Beat.*) Wait a minute. Get a grip, Jasper. Who are you talking to? . . . (*Beat. He gets out his iPhone.*) Siri, I think I need help with the French horn.

SOUND: voice of Siri.

Siri I think, therefore I am. But let's not put Descartes before the horse.

Jasper What? Siri! I need French horn help!

SOUND: voice of Siri.

Siri I found three places matching 'French Horn Help'. French Horn Novelty Dildos. Paxman's Musical Instruments. 'British Horn Society Festival annual massed horn blow takes place this Sunday . . .'

Jasper Wings to fly . . .

Blackout.

SOUND: Handel's Hallelujah Chorus, merging with the British Horn Society massed horn blow.

Jasper metamorphoses into Dave Lee, veteran hornsman.

Dave Welcome, welcome, welcome to the British Horn Society, for those of you who haven't been before! Yes, a fair few new faces out there, as well as some of the old. Hello, Bernard. My name's Dave, Dave Lee, and I'm from the People's Republic of Yorkshire. Currently residing in the orchestra pit of London's *Les Misérables*. Have to say, it's a bit of a thrill for me to be conducting you all at this year's Massed Horn Blow! What a marvellous sight you all are! A horn armada on a sea of brass! And haven't we had a wonderful weekend so far, eh? It's been a right smorgasbord of recitals and concerts. My chops have had a proper workout, that's for sure. And I trust you're all coming to this year's finale concert tonight where our very own Margaret here will be filling this year's amateur slot by treating us to some of her Strauss One! Good luck, Margaret! We're right behind you. Trust you'll be wearing your special pants. I know I'll be wearing mine! But seriously, folks, trying to make music come out of one of these things is no laughing matter. But what do we actually know about the *history* of the French horn? Anybody?

Jasper Um . . . Jasper. Is it true, Dave, that an ancestor of the French horn blew down the walls of Jericho? In the Bible?

Dave Correct, Jasper! I wasn't expecting that one. I'll have to keep an eye on you! Yes, ladies and gentlemen, the horn is mankind's original instrument. It can be found in history in many different forms: the conch shell, the ram's horn, the Roman cornu, the Viking lur, the Tibetan schlong. (*Beat.*) I may have made that last one up. But they all have one thing in common: a column of air being blown through a conical shape.

SOUND: rogue horn blast.

Thank you, Bernard. Don't call us. Now, the first composer to welcome the French horn indoors with its mucky boots on were the great George Frederick Handel. And I adore Handel. Every time I walk into a room I just adore Handel. Now, I'd like to hear a bit more of that Hallelujah Chorus, eh? . . . So: embouchures at the ready, diaphragms full and perky, and let's take it from 'King of Kings'. (*Lifts his baton.*) Two, three, four!

SOUND: 'King of Kings' played by the massed horns.

Jasper (*over the music*) Here I am! I'm one of seventy French horns. Seventy! And we're playing. God we're playing. I am playing the French horn for the first time in thirty-nine years! My lip's going and I'm sounding crap – well I would be if I could hear myself! But it doesn't matter! I'm in there with all the other kamikaze amateurs on seventh horn! Sound flooding every surface, every pore. Split notes all over the place! (*Singing.*) 'For he shall reign forever and ever . . . King of Kings!' This is fantastic! 'And Lord of Lords!' This is what I've been searching for. For the first time in years I am elated!

And I don't want this to stop. I want more. (*An idea.*) Hey! Wait – wait a minute. I could start again. Yes. I could take up the horn again. In fact . . . not just take it up, I could take it *on*! I could come back here, next year. And not with Bernard or Margaret or anyone else on seventh horn. Just me on stage! Playing a solo! Star . . . of the British Horn Society!!

The music reaches its climax on his last line.

Play a solo? Who am I kidding? Why the hell would I want to do that? How the hell would I do that? In front of five hundred real French horn players? It's ridiculous. Preposterous! I don't know what came over me. I'm middle-aged. Mind you, so is Margaret . . .

(*Cheerily.*) Apparently, mid-life is the most miserable time of our lives. All those youthful ambitions just shrivel up and die. Like scoring that century at Lords. Taking part in an orgy. Finishing *Ulysses* . . . Starting *Ulysses*. No, it's hit me harder than I thought it would, this ageing thing. You know you're getting old when you look down and you see your shoelace has come undone, and you're about to bend down to tie it up when you stop and you think to yourself: 'Hang on, if I wait till the *other* one comes undone, I'll only have to bend down the once . . . ' The fact is, ladies and gentlemen, none of us are going to get out of this alive. Did you get that memo? It's downhill all the way to the crematorium, folks! And yet . . . something's stirring. I can feel a tectonic plate with my name on it . . . shifting. The past is calling to me.

SOUND: Sibelius Fifth Symphony.

I don't know where obsession comes from. I just know it's rising up, engulfing me. Resistance is futile. So now I'm listening to music all the time. Classical music. Horn music. And I'm going to concerts. Loads and loads of concerts. And there's one Prom at the Albert Hall that makes me feel like I'm fifteen again . . .

The music surges.

I'm surrounded by students . . . music students, mostly. And we're listening . . . just listening, to the sounds of a youth orchestra. I'm in floods before they even play a note. All that talent! All that hope!

The music crescendoes.

Well, it wasn't all horns . . . there were a couple of trombones in there somewhere. (*Beat.*) Why did Sibelius produce nothing for the last thirty years of his life except silence? What a waste. And why do I, now, feel this need to make some kind of noise? My life used to stretch out before me like this vast ocean of opportunity. But now I'm sinking like a stone, gone, out of sight. No trace that I was ever here at all. Just a few ripples left on the surface and that's it. I've done nothing to make my life memorable, nothing. Oh, look, having children doesn't count. It certainly doesn't help.

Jasper morphs into Daniel, his teenage son.

Daniel What do you mean I don't count?

Jasper Daniel! Of course you count! I just mean . . . it's not exactly an achievement to have a child . . . in itself. *Per se.*

Daniel Great. Thanks. It's not exactly an achievement living on your own in a dump either, Mr Successful.

Jasper Yes, well, it's modest. It's all I can afford right now. But it's very convenient for the Underground.

Daniel You mean it goes right through your kitchen?

Jasper Which also means it's very easy for you to come and visit. Come as often as you want. (*Beat.*) Anyway, how are you, Daniel?

Daniel Fine.

Jasper And?

Daniel And what?

Jasper How's school?

Daniel Fine.

Jasper How's your mum?

Daniel Will you stop interrogating me? I thought you said you had Xbox.

Jasper Do you want to know how I am?

Daniel Well, I can see how you are, durr.

Jasper Oh Daniel, I just want you to . . . for us to . . . (*Losing his patience.*) Look, I'm sorry but I can't take you seriously with your trousers like that – can you just pull them up a bit? Like another foot? And do something with your fringe. I can't see your face –

Daniel Don't touch my hair! God, you're like so weird. Mum's right.

  Daniel exits.

Jasper Daniel? Come back! Daniel! Hang on, what do you mean, your mum's right? Daniel! (*Beat. He sits with the Horn.*) How did I let this happen? Was *I* like that as a teenager?

Horn Yes.

Jasper What?

Horn Yes!

Jasper Really?

Horn You forget. I was there. You want truth? You was worse.

Jasper Rubbish. What do you know?

Horn Too much, maybe? Otherwise, why you hide from me all these years? And why you let your boy talk to you like this?

Jasper Now look, I don't know what's going on here, but I do not need advice from a talking horn!

Horn We used to be so close! Make music, play concerts.

Jasper Aren't you forgetting something?

Horn Gah! One school concert car crash and *s'plocha!* No thank you, no goodbye. Nothing. School concert solo was not so bad!

Jasper (*incensed*) Now you listen to me: I had post-traumatic stress for years after that concert. *Years!*

SOUND: an underground train crashes through his kitchen.

Jasper rummages in a cardboard box of ancient vinyl.

My classical vinyl collection. All the great horn players. The Aussie, Barry Tuckwell. Hermann Baumann, recorded the Mozart horn concertos four times. Dennis Brain! The legend, the one and only! (*Finding more stuff.*) Wedding photos! Does one keep wedding photos when you're . . . ? School reports! Bizarre, what we keep and what we throw away, isn't it? Music! (*Reads.*) 'Jasper has been practising well. A little more self-confidence in his playing would be better.' (*Reads another.*) 'Jasper's playing would benefit from an injection of self-confidence.' (*A third.*) 'A little more self-confidence . . . No doubt joining the school orchestra will help to bring this on.' Ha! The school orchestra!

SOUND: noisy school orchestra tuning up.

Mr Cartledge (*bringing the orchestra to order*) Thank you. THANK YOU! Thank you, everybody. Now everybody, this is Jasper. You're over there, at the back, next to Francis. You'll have to snuggle up, I'm afraid. We're rather pushed for room. Timpani, can you accommodate? Two French horns at last! How mellifluous! I believe it was Robert Schumann who said, 'The horn is the soul of the orchestra!'

Jasper Our conductor, Mr . . . Mr . . . Cartledge!! Yes, old Ligament! He was impossibly tall. And I couldn't get over him using my first name. A master, calling me 'Jasper'? What was he doing being all matey? Anyway, I'm sitting next to Francis who is a total and utter nerd. Year above, I think. Black greasy hair, and terrible B.O. Or is that me? (*To Francis.*) Alright? First horn? (*Indicates himself.*) Second horn. (*Scrutinising the music.*) Something by Schu . . . bert. (*To Francis.*) Oi, are they all called Schu-something? (*Looks at the score.*) Doesn't look too difficult. Give or take the odd flurry of squiggles.

Mr Cartledge Now . . . Schubert's Ninth was, in fact, his Seventh. Which is really rather amusing when you think about it. It is generally referred to as the Great C Major. But to we musicians of the *cognoscenti* it will always be 'The Great Sea Monster'!

Jasper I wasn't really listening. I was giving the music a once-over, translating dots into fingerings. Open, one and two, two. Bloody hell! The room is teeming, heaving with . . . girls! There's got to be at least . . . three! Including one with an unbelievably big violin between her legs. Oh, she's beautiful. She looks just like Lady Di! Oops. She catches me staring at her. Quick – empty the water. It's spit actually. Puddles of gob everywhere, like you've peed yourself. Disgusting. Occupational hazard though. First, you've got to find it. Then you've got to . . . get rid of it.

He pulls a slide out of the horn and vigorously shakes it, accidentally flicking water into his eye.

I'll play quietly. Skirt along the edge of the noise. Keep out of harm's way. Old Ligament raises his stick. And on the first beat I copy Smelly. (*Raises his horn.*) By the second beat the horn is safely to my lips. On the third beat, I look around and notice that no one else in the entire room is playing, no one else that is apart from Smelly. By the fourth beat, I'm having a minor coronary. The Great C Major, it turns out, begins with a solo for horns. A SORN HOLO!

Mr Cartledge Second horn? Are you with us?

Jasper (*standing up*) Um . . . er . . . I'm not quite sure, sir.

Mr Cartledge Once more!

SOUND: Schubert's Great C Major horn solo.

Jasper tries and fails to play along.

Mr Cartledge (*patience itself*) It's in C major, Jasper.

Jasper It's what, sir?

Mr Cartledge The Great C Major is written in . . . ? (*Aside.*) Settle down strings. (*To Jasper.*) C Major. You'll have to transpose.

Jasper Do what, sir?

Mr Cartledge Transpose, Jasper. Transpose.

Jasper Transpose to what, sir?

Mr Cartledge The C is really a G. You have to drop every note you see on the page by a fourth. (*Beat.*) A fourth? Four notes, Jasper! (*Sings.*) Do, re, mi, fa!

Jasper (*appalled*) What, *all of it*? (*To the audience.*) Suddenly, before my eyes, an entire sheet of music is morphing into incomprehensible hieroglyphs. Tadpoles thrown randomly onto the page! In theory this should be easy – you can only play one note at a time. Unfortunately, when it comes to the French horn, nothing is ever easy. Turns out there are two ways of 'transposing'. Either the publisher can do it, therefore preventing a lot of grief, pain, and tears. Or the horn player has to do it right there and then, on his own, in his head, ON THE SPOT! And the great news for budding horn players everywhere is that a precedent was established in the nineteenth century which meant that horn players would just have to lump it! But do you know what? Most of them actually love it! Sets them apart, you see. Makes them feel like they've got an extra mountain to climb! (*Beat.*) And then there was the counting! Whole afternoons of just counting!

I'd get lost as a matter of course. Eighty-seven bars rest! I'm losing the will to live. Ooh – a couple of notes! Missed those. *A hundred and three bars rest!!* What's wrong with these people? Don't they want the horns to join in? Concentrate, Jasper, two, three, four. Don't look at her, two, three, four. As she sways from side to side, two, three, four. (*Beat.*) I can see her bra strap! (*Looks back to the sheet music.*) Bollocks, I've lost it again! But then the time signature would change. We've gone into five-eight. Why? WHY? What the hell's five-eight?!

Mr Cartledge Second horn! WHERE ARE YOU?!?

Jasper (*still reading school reports*) 'Another excellent term for Jasper. By all accounts he is turning into a very solid ensemble player.' Solid!? 'And he has made great strides with the Mozart Horn Concerto.' (*Beat.*) Mozart . . . ?

SOUND: Mozart Flute Concerto, K.313.

Mr Cartledge (*a knock*) Ah! Do come in, Jasper, come in, take a pew. Now, I thought it was about time we had a little *chattette à deux* about your development. (*He's holding music.*) I've been musing over this long and hard and I've decided to give you something really rather special. D'you know what it is?

Jasper Music, sir?

Mr Cartledge Yes of course it's music. But it's not just any music, Jasper. It's Wolfie!

Jasper What?

Mr Cartledge Wolfgang.

Jasper Who?

Mr Cartledge Wolfgang Amadeus Mozart! You've heard of him, surely? He without whom life simply wouldn't be worth living. I thought it was about time we let you loose on a musical masterpiece. Mozart's third horn concerto in E flat major, Köchel 447.

Jasper Kirk who??

Mr Cartledge Köchel! 447! Now . . . Mozart's four horn concertos are the base camp of the repertoire. Slog your way up to base camp, and from there you can dream of conquering anything. Even the daunting peaks of Strauss and Mahler. Mozart composed number three for his old family friend, Josef Leutgeb, who was the greatest horn player of his day. And perhaps Vienna's finest cheese-monger – which is a detail I really rather relish.

Now, number three follows the traditional concerto structure of its period: three movements – Allegro, Larghetto, Allegro. A quick opening movement, followed by a slower middle movement, before the pace picks up again with a rollicking hunting tune for the finale. Oh you're going to absolutely love it, Jasper. But here's the really fascinating fact: the Larghetto is better known as the *Romanze*. Because that's the word Mozart actually scribbled on Leutgeb's manuscript. Imagine that! *Romanze!* And that's what I'm hoping for, for you, Jasper. That you will have your very own *romanze* with K.447. I remember the day my own music master, Dr Tuft, gave me my first grown-up challenge: a Mozart flute concerto. Number one in G. K.313. Dear old Tufty. That music has stayed with me at my side through thick and thin, a true friend. And if you're as lucky as I was with K.313, K.447 will live with you and bless you for the rest of your life. And of course you know what the secret is, don't you? The three Ps. Practice. Practice and . . .

Jasper Practice, sir?

Mr Cartledge No, actually – it's patience.

Blackout.

SOUND: *Mozart K.447 Romanze.*

Jasper *(holding the music)* Romanze? That's not quite how I remember it. Well, there's only one way to find out. Here goes!

(*Beat.*) Wait a minute. What am I *doing*? I can't play this! I can't read music anymore. And what's the fingering? The horn's in F. But this is in E flat. Is that a tone up? Or a tone down? And if I hold the thumb key down then because it's a double horn, that means I'm in B flat . . .? Oh, bloody hell. (*Distressed.*) It's tadpoles again!

Horn Er, excuse me, please? May I make comment?

Jasper No.

Horn Cut yourself slack, mister. We play Hallelujah horn blow, seventh horn, *very* nice!

Jasper Rubbish. I split more notes than I hit.

Horn Little rusty, maybe. But we have a good time, yes?

Jasper Maybe. But I'm too old to start again.

Horn You say you want play solo like Margaret. Be star of British Horn Society! Margaret not too old!

Jasper Yes but Margaret can *play*!

Horn *You* can play – with help! We play together. We play Mozart 447!

Jasper No! Absolutely not!

Horn Yes! Why not? We make it different. Better!

Jasper You can't change the past!

Horn Not change past – heal present.

Jasper Right. That's it. It's eBay for you! (*Putting horn back in the case.*)

Horn Sure, eBay! Great idea! LOSER! QUITTER!

Jasper (*his eye sees something*) Hang on, what was that?

Horn (*from inside case*) COWARD!

He opens the case just enough to retrieve Dave Lee's business card.

19

Jasper (*slams lid*) SHUT UP! (*Reads.*) 'Dave Lee. British Horn Society.' I can't call Dave Lee! (*Then again . . .*) Go on. Why not? What have you got to lose? (*Dials Dave's number.*) Hello, is that Dave?

SOUND: Dave's garbled voice on the phone.

Dave Lee? Hello, Dave! It's Jasper. We met at the British Horn Society? We had a few beers after the Hallelujah horn blow. Walls of Jericho question? Yes! Well, you see the thing is, Dave, I've had quite an interesting idea, and I was just wondering if I could run it by you? (*Beat.*) Well, I really need your advice.

Blackout.

SOUND: Mozart K.447, first movement.

Dave Don't do it.

Jasper What?

Dave You want my advice? Don't do it.

Jasper Why not?

Dave Takes bollocks of Sheffield steel to stand up and play that thing in public. It's the French horn, Jasper! Takes no prisoners. What do you want to put yourself through that for?

Jasper Well, Dave, I've reached that time in my life where I want to . . . need to . . . give myself a bit of a challenge.

Dave A 'challenge', eh? Why the Mozart?

Jasper I played it at school. I know it pretty well actually. Number three in E flat major. K.447.

Dave Well, I suppose it is the easy one. Make sure you hit that second note though. Tricky bugger, that D. You've got to dig it out. Da-*dah* . . .

Jasper Well obviously, Dave, I will be trying to hit *all* the right notes!

Dave Oh aye. So how can *I* help?

Jasper Well, I was wondering whether you could, you know, give me a quick . . . refresher?

Dave Oh. Righto. When d'you last play then?

Jasper It's a few years ago now.

Dave How many years ago?

Jasper Thirty-nine.

Dave Thirty . . . !? Christ-all-bloody-mighty! Well, you'd better get it out then.

Jasper What – now?

Dave Aye. You can give us a quick blast of K.447. (*He roars with mirth.*)

Jasper plays very badly, then returns the horn to its case.

Dave And you propose to inflict *that* on the audience of the British Horn Society?

Jasper I haven't approached them yet . . . but yes that is my plan. Obviously, I've got a bit of work to do . . .

Dave That, my friend, is the understatement of the century.

Jasper (*ashamed*) Yeah, you're right, Dave. Apologies. It's a stupid idea. (*Packing up.*) I got carried away after the Hallelujah horn blow. In fact the horn has started talking to me. Has that ever happened to you . . . ? No, I thought not. Anyway, thanks for your time, I'll see myself out –

Dave Hold yer horses. I'm not saying it's impossible. There is an amateur slot at the concert, where Margaret played the Strauss. But you'd have to audition, lad – and not for me, mind, but for the President of the British Horn Society, Sir Humphrey Crutwell – or God, as he prefers to be called. And frankly, right now, you are a million miles away from auditioning.

But tell you what, I'm not averse to a bit of a 'challenge' myself, so . . . let's have a look at that instrument of yours. (*Jasper hands Dave the horn.*) Crikey! (*He checks the maker's mark.*) Thought so. Czechoslovakian. Drop that, they'd have to fix the floor. Alright then, Jasper. Back to basics. Purse your lips. Keep your cheeks in check and make a buzzing sound. Let's have a look at that embouchure.

Jasper feebly obliges.

Dave Bloody hell! You're going to need more than a refresher. You're going to need proper lessons. Intensive. And you'll have to practise like buggery. You'll not even get out of the traps without a cast iron warm-up. You are going need the bible.

Jasper The bible?

Dave (*retrieving a copy of Farkas*) The bible. Philip Farkas. Born Chicago, 1914. Happily played the tuba – or at least he did until one day a streetcar driver says to him, 'You can't bring that thing on board. It's too big – it's blocking the gangway.' He points to another bandsman's instrument: 'I don't mind them ones; you can bring one of them on board.' By the age of twenty-two he were principal horn of the Chicago Symphony Orchestra. Imagine that, eh? Twenty-two! And all thanks to a bloody tram driver! And then, Jasper, he wrote the bible. In the beginning there was Farkas. And Farkas saith unto the horn player: thou shalt practise thy scales, arpeggios, slurring, fingering, tonguing, trilling, vibratos, tremolos, stilettos, pedalos, lilos, avocados, peccadillos . . . It's got the lot!

Jasper Very good, Dave. So how often would I need to, you know . . . with this bible?

Dave Every time you play, Jasper. Which should of course be every day! I have for the past 40,000 years. And if you're going to climb Mount Everest in front of the British Horn Society then I'm buggered if you're going to get out of it!

Jasper So, you mean Dave . . . this could actually happen?

Dave I might be persuaded to make a phone call or two, get you on the audition list – if I thought you were serious, and prepared to do the work. And that's where Farkas comes in. Two hours' warm-up with the bible every day – yes, *every day.* Only then can you reward yourself with ten minutes' fun.

Jasper Fun?

Dave With the Mozart! Oh aye, you've got to have fun on the horn, Jasper. Or you'd kill yourself! (*Dave laughs his mad laugh.*) Right! Pub!

Blackout.

SOUND: London pub ambience. The horns from 'Sgt. Pepper' in the background.

Dave (*in his cups, mid-anecdote*) So I says to Von Caravan, I says, 'What's the difference, Herbert, between an orchestra and a bull?' 'Tell me pleeze!' he says. So I says, 'On a bull, Herbert, the horns are at the *front,* and the arsehole's at the *back!*' No, he didn't find it very funny either. (*Beat.*) So tell me, Jasper, how do you make a crust?

Jasper I write, Dave. I'm a writer.

Dave Ooh, you write do you? And what d'you write about?

Jasper Oh, you know.

Dave No, I don't know.

Jasper Features, profiles, interviews, that sort of thing. Other people's adventures.

Dave So this musical bungee jump's your latest assignment then, is it?

Jasper Actually no, Dave. It's me trying to have my own adventure.

Dave Ah! Midlife crisis!

Jasper Well . . .

Dave Divorced?

Jasper Er . . .

Dave Kids?

Jasper Yeah. Boy. Fifteen.

Dave How's he taken it?

Jasper Well, you know. It's a process.

Dave That bad, eh? I've got a son too. He don't talk to me either, and he's thirty-bloody-three.

Jasper Oh, I'm sorry, Dave. What happened?

Dave Divorce! Occupational hazard. Married to the bloody instrument. Cheers! (*Drinks from his pint.*) Have I put you off yet?

Jasper Dave, I feel as though I've failed at everything. Everything that really matters. My marriage. My son. Myself. I badly need to succeed at something. And I know it seems insane, but I think this . . . could be it. Playing a solo at the finale concert of the British Horn Society.

Dave You're mad. D'you know that?

Jasper Yes, Dave. So, tell me about this audition.

Dave Well you'd have to play something – some of the Mozart. Slow movement would do. Only one snag. The auditions are next week!

Blackout.

SOUND: two opening chords of Schumann's Konzertstück.

Jasper Next week!? I can't eat, I can't sleep. It's flipping Farkas day-and-night.

He attempts a phrase on the horn.

SOUND: *his neighbours start banging on the wall.*

Neighbours WILL YOU SHUT UP?!

Jasper (*ignoring the banging*) Again.

Jasper plays the phrase again.

SOUND: *more banging and yelling.*

Jasper Again!

He plays the phrase again.

SOUND: *neighbours thumping and yelling.*

SOUND: *Dave's voice in Jasper's tortured mind.*

Dave An amateur practises till he gets it right. A professional practises until he doesn't get it wrong!

SOUND: *police siren, then all sounds merging until pierced by the Siegfried horn call.*

Jasper and Dave are waiting for Jasper's audition.

Sir Humphrey Jason! Jason!?

Jasper This is it, Dave. Any last-minute tips?

Dave Knock him dead.

Sir Humphrey Ah, Jason.

Jasper It's Jasper, sir.

Sir Humphrey Sir Humphrey Crutwell, Jason, President of the British Horn Society. Do come through. (*To Dave.*) Not you, Dave.

Dave (*aside*) Brasshole.

Sir Humphrey (*deaf*) WHAT?

Blackout.

SOUND: *Schumann's Konzertstück.*

Jasper Well, there was *one* positive about the audition. Dave didn't tell me Sir Humphrey was deaf! (*Beat.*) Weird auditioning for something at my age. (*Looks at his watch.*) Come on, Dave, where are you?!

(*Picks up the horn.*) Why is it I'm prepared to hammer away at this thing now . . . but I just couldn't get it when I was 15?

SOUND: 'Liebestod' from Tristan und Isolde.

I blame the girl with the big violin between her legs. That's what it boils down to, doesn't it? The first thing to be consumed in the gushing molten lava of teenage, angst-ridden lust is . . . the instrument!

Jasper But this time, I'm in love. *I AM IN LOVE!!* (*He dances with the horn.*)

The music stops suddenly. Jasper wheels round in surprise.

Jasper (*defensive*) What?

Daniel (*horrified*) Dad, that is so *gay*.

Jasper Actually it's *not* 'gay', Daniel. And even if it was, there's nothing wrong with that. Look, I don't expect you to understand. But after a very difficult period of my life, I've finally found something that I love, that is for *me*. And I am not ashamed to say: this is who I am.

Daniel Oh shit, you really *are* gay! Why are you doing this at, like, your age?

Jasper It's making music, Daniel! *Proper* music. With heart and soul and passion. Not that awful rapping, thrashing noise you inflict on yourself.

Daniel I don't get it. First you split up with Mum, then you like sell our house. What the hell's next?

Jasper Well actually, Daniel, I'm hoping to play a solo. In a concert. With an orchestra! Mozart's third horn concerto. And I'd love you to come and support me.

Daniel (*appalled*) What!? A solo? Why?

Jasper Well, when I was your age, Dan, I played the French horn. But I didn't practise. And I regret that now so –

Daniel Oh my God! Mum's right. (*Storms out.*)

Jasper Daniel! Daniel! Come back! What do you mean, 'Mum's right'?

Dave enters, only just avoiding collision with departing Daniel.

Dave Eh up, you must be Daniel! (*To Jasper.*) He looks just like you! . . . Everything all right?

Jasper Hi, Dave. I just told him about the audition. But it didn't go down quite as well as I'd hoped. (*Beat.*) So tell me: what did Sir Humphrey say? Did I get it?

Dave Get what?

Jasper The concert! The amateur slot!

Dave Oh that. We won't know about that for a few months yet.

Jasper WHAT!?

Dave Oh aye. He's seeing at least half a dozen others. You didn't think you were the only nutjob out there, did you?

Jasper But Dave! How can I keep this up if I don't know whether they are going to let me do it or not? I really need this! My lips are shredded. I've had a warning from the landlord because of the noise. Even my son thinks I'm crap.

Dave Well, you were the one that wanted – what was it? A bit of a 'challenge'? I never said it were going to be easy. But you're making it harder for yourself! It's not nuclear bloody fusion. Get a grip, Jasper. You've got to find a way of enjoying the climb, without losing yer marbles in the meantime. (*Genius.*) Hey, I tell you what! I've had an idea!

Blackout.

SOUND: Haydn's 'Hornsignal' Symphony fanfare gives way to the engine of a jumbo jet, then the sounds of nature in which snippets of Bruckner, Mahler, Beethoven and Strauss are heard in the distance.

Jasper enters in Hawaiian shirt and baseball cap, with his horn and a battered suitcase.

Jasper Horn camp! I'll say it again. HORN CAMP! Yes, there is such a place. And where else would it be but in . . . America! Camp Ogontz, deep in the rolling Adirondacks of New Hampshire. There's a silver lake, a babbling brook, the sound of offstage horns everywhere.

Kelly-Ann Gee, I just *love* your accent! Would you say that again?

Jasper (*James Bond-style*) Hullo! My name's Jasper. From London, England.

Kelly-Ann Hi, Jasper from London, England. I'm Kelly-Ann from Athens, Georgia.

Jasper It's as if I've died and gone to heaven – horn heaven! The only difference is that I thought once you got into heaven the auditioning was over.

Jasper drops his luggage upstage and returns as Kendall Betts.

Kendall Heeeey! Real glad you made it! How're y'all doing? Kendall Betts!

Jasper Kendall Betts. Principal horn of the Minnesota Orchestra. It's the induction and I'm in a log cabin with Kelly-Ann, a grumpy old sod from Florida who's got to be at least eighty, and Sister Monica, a nun from Massachusetts. Oh and it turns out Kendall's a bit of a comedian.

Kendall So, who's up first? Jasper, you wanna show us how it's done in the good ol' UK of England?

Jasper Sorry? You want me to play *now?*

Kendall Since you're here! I just want to get a feel for the level you're all at right now.

Jasper But Kendall, I haven't done my Farkas warm-ups. And I have been travelling for over fifteen hours...

Kendall Oh, you'll be great. Really! There's no pressure, absolutely none at all. The bar is *way* down here. (*Kendall indicates a high bar.*) You go right ahead. I'll get the earplugs!

Jasper I play.

Kendall (*in mild shock*) Oooooo. Yeeaaah. Ouch! So what exactly are you hoping to achieve at Horn Camp, Jasper? 'Cause you sure as hell gotta work on that airflow, buddy. You've got sixteen feet of tubing to work through. You gotta find the sweet spot. If it feels like you're trying to take a crap, that's probably what it's gonna sound like.

Jasper Well, to be perfectly honest with you, Kendall, I've been told I need a bit of match practice, that's all.

Kendall Pardon me?

Jasper I've been invited to perform at the British Horn Society. A solo, actually. And I've been told I just need a bit of performance practice.

Kendall Well, I hear you. But I'm not sure that's such a good idea. We do have a concert at the end of the week. But if you crash and burn . . .

Jasper Kendall, it's now or never for me. I've just spent fifteen hundred bucks getting here. I'm prepared to take the risk.

Kendall They ever let you play in public before?

Jasper Yes! I played K.447 at school when I was a kid.

Kendall Really!? How'd it go?

Jasper (*fibbing*) Like a dream.

Kendall Well, if you're not ready for primetime, you're just not going to play. We've had *incidents* in the past, Jasper. You wouldn't want that – and we wouldn't want to listen! Horn Camp rules: bite off what you can chew! But if you still want to play in the concert, first you have to try out for Hermann . . .

Jasper Hermann?

Kendall Hermann Baumann.

Jasper Hermann-the-greatest-German-horn-player-since-the-war-Baumann?

Kendall Yeah! You know him? He's a sweetie.

Hermann materialises, a terrifying Teutonic maestro.

Hermann Und so, Yasper, from London, England. Vas you are playing?

Jasper (*awestruck*) I'm attempting the 447.

Hermann Vas?

Jasper The 447?

Hermann Is not ze autobahn.

Jasper I'm sorry?

Hermann You make it sound like a road number!

Jasper Hermann Baumann. Turns out at the age of sixty he had a stroke, lost his speech, everything. Slowly, though, over the last ten years, he's put the pieces of his life back together and returned to teaching.

Hermann Und so, Yasper. Vee begin, ja? With ein biiig breath!

Jasper Now the first movement, the Allegro, is rather more testing than the Romanze. It's got a couple of unsolved problems for me. First of all, it's got a lot of trills. And I can't do trills. But that's nothing compared to the bigger problem of my cadenza – that's the freestyle bit where you show off. I haven't got one. Or at least I didn't have, until last night, when in the privacy of my log cabin, Sister Monica helped me knock this one up for Hermann.

Jasper plays what sounds like a phrase from Phantom of the Opera *bolted onto the Romanze.*

Hermann (*horrified*) Stop, stop, stop! Vas ist das?

Jasper My cadenza, Hermann. It's a lyrical tribute to Andrew Lloyd –

Hermann Rubbish! You understand? *Rubbish!* Where you find zis?

Hermann studies the music, muttering.

Jasper (*helpful*) Would you like me to have aniother go?

Hermann No. *No.* No! (*Undoing his shirt.*)

Jasper It's getting really hot now, and Hermann is completely . . . unbuttoned.

Hermann Mein Gott! (*Staring at Jasper's copy of the Mozart.*) Vas ist das?

Jasper It's the fingerings, Hermann.

Hermann Ja, ja, I know iz ze fingerings! Why? *Why?* WHY!?

Jasper From when I played it school, when I was a kid.

Hermann (*aghast*) You play ze whole concerto and you not know ze fingerings?! (*German expletives.*) We move on, ja? To ze third movement. Ze Rondo. Ze hunting tune. (*Jasper prepares to play.*) No, no! First you zing.

Jasper I'm sorry?

Hermann First you zing!

Jasper Do *what*?

Hermann Zing! (*He points at the music.*) From here.

Confused, Jasper lamely sings the beginning of the Rondo.

Jasper La la la la la la la la la la, la –

Hermann No! No! No! Das ist scheisser! You zing from *here*. (*Grabs his crotch.*) La la la la la la la la la la (*etc.*) Zat is zinging! You understand? You *learn*! First you zing. *Then* you play.

Reluctantly Jasper grabs his own crotch.

Jasper La la la la la la la la la la la la – I look and feel like an utter tit.

He spits the final la las furiously at Hermann.

Hermann Gut. Is bedder, ja? Und now, lift up your horn, und – No! Up. Up! *UP!!* Hold it like a man!

Jasper (*distressed*) I am!!

Hermann Ja! JA! JA! Now you *find* him, your inside hornsman! Look at Kelly-Ann und Sister Monica! Zey are vimmin. But zey play like vild men! Und so, stop your crybaby! Lift up your horn und play, Mr James Bond!

Blackout.

SOUND: the wailing horns of the James Bond theme gives way to crickets and a Rossini natural horn solo.

Jasper (*flat on his back*) It's just so bloody *hard* playing this thing. And it's . . . so hot!

Kelly-Ann Hey Jasper. Whatcha doin' hidin' away there in the long grass?

Jasper Oh, hi Kelly-Ann. I don't know. Licking my wounds.

Kelly-Ann Come on now. You did pretty good. Hermann let you off easy.

Jasper Really? It's a long way to come to be quite so humiliated.

Kelly-Ann Well, I guess you just gotta find that wild man lurking in there, like me and Sister Monica!

Jasper That's not quite how we do things in the good old UK of England.

Kelly-Ann How long since you like blowed on that old Lídl anyway?

Jasper How old are you, Kelly-Ann?

Kelly-Ann Me? Twenty-nine.

Jasper In that case, I haven't played the horn since before you were born.

Kelly-Ann Wow dawg! That is just awesome!! Hey! I know what you need: you need some natural therapy! You taken a class yet with Lowell Greer? He's that big ol' bear wandering round camp, handing out pearls of wisdom and homegrown CDs.

SOUND: birdsong then a Rossini natural horn ensemble.

Lowell Welcome to nature's classroom, friends. This is where I like to work. Where we let it all hang out. And this, Jasper, is for you.

Lowell hands Jasper a horn.

Jasper Gosh thanks, Lowell. What is it?

Lowell It's a hunting horn.

Jasper Ah. It's got no valves!

Lowell Yeah, I know. I gave it a valvectomy. Welcome to the ensemble, friend.

Jasper I enjoy myself more than I can say. Being back in a band, part of 'something'. And I realise what it is I love about the horn. It's being a cog in a wheel. I don't like being the whole machine.

Lowell Hey Jas, come over here. Take the weight off your lips. (*Lowell hands him a bottle of water.*) You know, as our playing skills develop, so too do our powers of critical observation. Especially when we're trying to re-kindle those past glories of youth. We tend to dwell on every failure. Why is that? Why don't we dwell our triumphs? I think all horn players should be given a pill – a partial-lobotomy pastille. . . Hitting all those darn notes? It's a numbers game out there. In quantity operations there will be losses. So . . . part of what we practise is confidence. We create the illusion of aplomb. So stop screaming at yourself inside there. Relax. *Chill.* Surprise yourself. Pretend you're a good horn player.

Jasper Yes, Lowell! You're right. Thank you! (*Yelling to the hillsides.*) I AM GREAT HORN PLAYER!! ('*PLAYER*' *echoes back at him.*)

Lowell *Good.* You're a *good* horn player, let's start with that first, my friend. (*Pause.*) I'll let you into a little secret. People take the Mozart's horn concertos *way* too seriously. All that post-Wagnerian, breast-pounding lyricism. Flute players – now when *they* play Mozart, they have this *effervescence.* We're allowed to find that too. That's what Mozart and Leutgeb were all about. They were having a good time! Farkas once told me: 'You gotta hunt for the levity!' Hunt for the levity. I like that. And that's what you gotta do, Jas. You just gotta enjoy the ride.

Jasper Enjoy the ride. 'Enjoy the climb.' Where have I heard that before? But how do I do that? How can I learn to let go when I'm terrified of falling?

   SOUND: opening of the Glière Concerto.

Jasper Well, the last night concert belonged to Hermann. The old bull stood up and played. My God, he plays. The great Glière concerto. A soaring, swooning piece, heavily romantic.

34

Post-Wagnerian breast-pounding lyricism very much called for, as well as a massive pair of lungs and lightning fingers. It's an impossible challenge. But Hermann takes a 'big breath' – and hurls himself off the cliff . . . (*Jasper listens intently.*) It's the first time he's played it in thirteen years, since he had the stroke. It's spellbinding. And later, as we file out into the starlit night, I finally realise what it is that Hermann's been trying to drum into my skull. When it comes to the French horn there is no alternative to standing up and being counted. (*Almost triumphant.*) You have to face down your demons!

Blackout.

Glière gives way to applause, traffic, rain and tube train.

Jasper enters sporting a horn camp T-shirt.

Jasper Hey, Daniel! Horn camp was magical. I did nothing but play the French horn all day. My lip is so strong now I could blow all night. It was like a horn Hogwarts!

Daniel You didn't seriously wear that, did you?

Jasper Yeah, isn't it great? I got one for you too. And I hung out with people closer to your age than mine. And not just blokes. We were scuttling in and out of log cabins. Playing in the outdoors with Sister Monica – she was a nun! Blowing in my trunks! It was awesome. Horn Nirvana! Life-changing!

Daniel A nun blowing in your trunks?

Jasper No! –

Daniel You really are, like, going to do this – solo thing?

Jasper Of course I'm going to do it. That's what Horn Camp was all about! I'm match fit and ready to blow. And it would really mean everything to me if you were there.

Daniel I told you I'm not coming.

Jasper Why not?

Daniel I can't talk to you. My mum is right!

Jasper What is your mum so right about, Daniel?

Daniel You want to know? (*Heating up.*) You really want to know? You're just not there! You're not there any more, Dad. You've abandoned me.

Jasper Abandoned you?

Daniel (*erupting*) Just let me finish, will you? Why is it always about you? Everything you do just makes things worse.

Jasper That wasn't my intention. I just want to make you proud of me.

Daniel Proud of you?! Why would I be proud of you making a tit of yourself, playing that thing in public? Just grow up will you? Admit it: that horn means more to you now than me.

Jasper Oh Daniel, that is outrageously dramatic! *You* grow up!

Daniel Oh, fuck off and die!

Blackout.

SOUND: Sir Humphrey's voice.

Sir Humphrey Dear Jasper, as I am sure you are aware there was fierce competition for the amateur slot for this year's finale concert . . .

Jasper . . . And I am afraid that on this occasion your audition has not been successful . . .

SOUND: more of Sir Humphrey's voice.

Sir Humphrey Please don't be discouraged, and by all means try again next year. In the meantime, keep blowing! Yours sincerely, Sir Humphrey Crutwell, President of the British Horn Society.

Jasper Fuck off and die.

SOUND: voice on the phone.

Caller Hello? Hello??

Jasper Sorry, not you! It's a Lídl. Full double. No, it's in good condition, just the usual wear and tear. Why am I selling? I'm having a clear out. Haven't got room for it anymore. Sure, you're welcome to come and have a blow. If you like it, make me an offer.

SOUND: snippet from John Williams' 'Funeral Pyre for a Jedi'.

Jasper picks up the horn.

Horn Why you quit? Why we stop make music?

Jasper Please. Enough. No more questions.

Horn You sell me, you have no wings to fly!

The music soars.

Jasper You can stop that!

The music ends rudely.

It's over. Deal with it. And this bloke's coming to buy you, so please cooperate and play nicely.

Horn British Horn Festival bullshit. Who they pick for solo?

Jasper I don't know. Bernard something-or-other.

Horn Bernard? *Bernard?* You mean beardy weirdo Bernard from Hallelujah horn blow?

SOUND: front door buzzer.

Dave (*excited*) Where have you *been*, Jasper? Why haven't you returned any of my calls?

Jasper Oh hi, Dave. What's the point? I've packed the whole thing in. I'm selling the horn. In fact, I thought you were the bloke coming to buy it now.

Dave Packed it in? What are you talking about? Listen to your messages, lad! You've got a concert to play in!

Jasper What?

Dave It's Bernard! (*Beat.*) He's had an accident.

Jasper An accident?

Dave He's pulled out. It's a long story. But Sir Humphrey got the reserve list out and your name were at the top.

Jasper (*disbelieving*) Me?

Dave Aye, you. (*Beat.*) Well why not you?

Jasper (*horrified*) Oh Dave, what have you done?

Dave Never you mind what I've done. You'll just have to tell this bloke that's coming you've changed your mind about selling. And let's get cracking. Don't just stand there. This is it!

Jasper Sorry, Dave. I can't.

Dave What do you mean you can't?

Jasper I can't do it.

Dave Course you can do it! What about all the hours we've put in? Horn Camp? Your son?

Jasper The horn's not right, Dave. I've got a bad feeling. Maybe next year . . .

Dave (*menacing*) Now you listen to me. I've broken every rule in the book to make this happen, and now you're trying every trick in the book to wriggle out of it?

Jasper Dave, you don't understand.

Dave Too bloody right I don't. So, *make* me understand. Before I punch your bloody lights out!

Jasper Look, when I said I performed K.447 at school, that isn't exactly strictly true.

Dave You what??

Jasper I was seventeen. I walked out onto the stage at our school music concert in front of hundreds of parents and boys, masters and . . . girls. And it was a public execution. A public disembowelling. My guts were spilling out all over that stage. I wanted to die. Quickly. But it was so slow. Three and a half minutes! I was *butchering* the Romanze. It was unrecognisable. My parents . . . I could feel their shame . . . the lights blinding me . . . sweat coursing down my face . . . melting. I battle on. But I can't shut that voice up. The voice in my head that's hating me, hating the noise I'm making. Please! Go away! Just let me die! Let this torment be over! (*Beat.*) And then I know exactly what I have to do. So, I roll my eyes, and, and . . .

Jasper faints, lies prone for a few moments, then sits up.

I didn't pick up the horn again for thirty-nine years. So you see, Dave, I can't do it. Not really. I'm a fraud. An impostor. I was gutless then, and I still am. (*Pause.*) I'm sorry I've wasted your time. . . . (*Reaching for his wallet.*) Please. Let me pay you for all your –

Dave (*slow hand-claps*) What a performance! I don't want your money, you bloody fool. Have you learned nothing from that French horn? That instrument has only given you your life back. Ever heard Dennis Brain play? Ever seen him perform? No, course you haven't. 'Cause he's dead! Driving home one night from a concert at the Edinburgh Festival, pushing himself too hard. Fell asleep at the wheel. Smacked into a tree. Killed. He were thirty-six. He never had the luxury of a midlife crisis. By the time he were your age he'd been dead twenty years!

Jasper You don't have to lecture me about Dennis Brain, Dave, I know all about Dennis . . .

Dave No! You don't know! Greatest horn player who ever lived. Whole nation mourned when he died. Seventy years ago. You want to make your mark? Pick it up. Go on. If you don't you'll regret it for the rest of your life. Every time you look in the mirror, you'll be looking into the eyes of a man who bottled it!

Blackout.

SOUND: 'The Ride of the Valkyries' ended by a needle-scratch.

Jasper (*munching on a banana*) For the nerves. Natural beta-blocker. (*Browses the festival programme.*) Oh my god! I'm on the bill between the President of the British Horn Society, and the horn section of the Berlin Phil! Oh, that's just perfect. Absolutely perfect! (*Beat.*) Uh oh. Here we go. Parched mouth? Here, sir. Nausea? Oh yeah. Heart pounding against rib cage? Yup. (*Beat.*) Hang on. What's this?? This is new! (*Clutching at his collar.*) I can't breathe! I've got to go out there and play and I can't breathe! *I'm having a heart attack!* Dave! Where are you, you bastard? Oh yes, he's out front, isn't he? Along with every other horn player in the country. And the ghost of Dennis Brain. (*Cries out.*) Help me, Dennis! What would Dennis Brain say to me right now? (*Pause.*) LOOK OUT! THERE'S A TREE!! No! He wouldn't say that! He'd say, 'Just go out and concentrate on what you know you can do. Don't worry about what you can't.' Yeah. That's good.

SOUND: the orchestra tuning up offstage.

Jasper Oh Christ. Oh Jesus! (*Pause.*) I'm on. (*Exits.*)

Blackout.

A moment or two later Jasper re-enters.

Jasper Ladies and gentlemen . . . distinguished members of the British Porn Society. (*Horrified by his error.*) I expect you're wondering who I am, and, indeed, what on earth I'm doing here. Well, I abandoned the French horn, this French horn, when I left school. To be honest, I was never very good. I didn't practise. But nearly forty years later, I felt an urgent need to take it up again. So I found my horn, from a country that no longer exists, and I went to play in last year's massed horn blow, conducted by Dave Lee. And in both senses of the word, had a *blast*. (*No one laughs.*) Anyway, to cut a long story short, I set myself the target of playing a solo at the festival a year on.

This festival. Now. (*Pause.*) So, I'd like to thank the British *Horn* Society, for giving me this opportunity. And Bernard, get well soon. Anything genuinely musical you hear in the next few minutes is down to Dave. Any errors are my own. And trust me there will be errors. Oh, and one more thing. I'd like to dedicate this performance to my son, Daniel, who can't be here today . . . Thank you.

Jasper puts music on the stand and prepares himself.

SOUND: Orchestral back for the K.447 Romanze.

Jasper plays. It's disastrous.

Jasper Fuck, fuck, fuck, fuck! SHIT! . . . How could I have missed the easiest note in the entire fucking piece? It sounds fucking appalling! Concentrate, Jasper!

He plays again. It's a mess.

I couldn't hit a cow's arse with a banjo!

He plays again. It's awful.

It's a catastrophe! There is only one thing for it. I'm just going to have to faint. But I'll have wasted a year of my life. (*In the voice of Dave Lee.*) You've got to have fun on the horn, Jasper! (*Kendall Betts.*) Find the sweet spot! (*Lowell Greer.*) Hunt for the levity! (*Hermann Baumann.*) BREATHE UND ZING!

Jasper takes a big breath. The phrase comes out OK. He celebrates like a golfer who just holed a forty-foot putt. He swells in confidence, almost dancing. The Romanze continues to the end without further incident, and he visibly grows in confidence.

Jasper Halfway. Empty the water. (*Beat.*) Hang on. Where's the terror? It's gone . . .

Horn Just play. Play heart out. Doesn't matter what comes out other end. Important thing is you have a go. We try your best. And no one – no one *ever* take this away.

SOUND: K.447 Rondo – Jasper plays more or less beautifully.

SOUND: applause.

Jasper What a thrill! What a buzz! I'm still shaking. Cracked a few notes but it didn't matter. I was up there, on the high wire, without a net. And did you hear those trills?! Quite like to do it again, actually. What shall we do next? Beethoven? Strauss? What do you think? (*No reply from the horn.*) Hmm? You probably want to do more Mozart, don't you? What do you think . . . ? (*No reply.*) Hey I'm talking to you! (*Beat. He hugs the horn with feeling.*) Thank you!

SOUND: a bright knock at the dressing room door.

Jasper Come in, Dave! So, what did you think of the –

Jasper sees it's not Dave but Daniel.

Daniel! (*Beat.*) Hi.

Daniel Hi.

Jasper Were you out there?

Daniel Yeah. I decided to come, actually. Bit last minute. (*Beat.*) You know, Dad, you really are a bit of a nutter.

Jasper Yes. Thanks for coming.

Daniel That's alright. (*Beat.*) You know you said 'British Porn Society'?

Jasper Yes. Yes, I know.

Beat.

Daniel Do you, like, wanna go for a drink or something?

Jasper What, now?

Daniel Yeah.

Jasper Okay! You buying?

Daniel Yeah. If you lend me twenty quid.

Jasper You go ahead. I'll catch you up.

Jasper watches Daniel leave.

SOUND: final chords of Sibelius Fifth Symphony.

He puts the horn in its case, blows it a kiss and leaves.

Light falls on the horn.

Blackout.